The Roe From Head To Toe

Written and compiled by : -

Victor Marshall McCurry.

First Published June 2000
Published by Victor Marshall McCurry.

All copyrights reserved by
Victor Marshall McCurry.

Cover design, paintings and illustrations
by Victor Marshall McCurry.

Special thanks to Deanna, my wife and friend
for all her hard work in the layout of this book.

ISBN 0-9538459-0-7

By the Same Author:
No Room for Ghosts.

Paintings

Illustrations

Introduction.

Standing along the banks of the river Roe, on any yard of its length, the angler, the poet, the artist or the tourist can enjoy the present and perhaps its history. Even an overcast sky should not deter the enthusiastic rambler from pursuing his enquiry along the glens of the river.

The path you walked has been a familiar haunt to our ancestors – Neolithic man – the Druids – Cruithni (Picts) – Celts – Vikings – Normans – English, Scotch, Welsh – they are all gone, or perhaps not, but the path is still here. The river flows on and the fish return each year but time has stood solid, or so it seems, as you survey the rocks on the banks, the trees shrouding the water and the momentary glimpse of a silver fish turn in the current.

This magical moment, as you walk up the path, meant the same to the "beaker people" (the same race that erected Stonehenge 3500 B.C.), with the instinct, reverence and skill to catch a fish. Their craft and ability were the same as yours, however the tackle was not as simply procured. The earliest inhabitants, locally, are recorded, as most agree, 7000 B.C. and the extent or the expanse of the river in those days encourages our imagination to wander.

When the O'Connors came north from Cashel, in the south, to invade the Roe Valley area in 568 A.D. they found a paradise and here they settled to farm and enjoy their new found freedom.

The O'Connors fought for this freedom to harvest the rich soil that they planted – the woodlands and forests that provided timber to build the framework for their huts with wattle and mud walls. The "bogs" constituted an abundance of turf to cook the silver salmon and trout in summer, along with a great variety of wildfowl and game. It is understood that for five hundred years they enjoyed this earned privilege – that is until the O'Cahans came along. But the

O'Connors left us their legacy from the name – Cinnighta or Cianachta and O'Conchobhair – anglicised to Kennaught. The O'Cahans were descended from the Connors/ O'Connors.

The O'Cahans completed their territorial arena by the expansion of areas outside the Roe Valley over the next five hundred years – a great number of O'Connors remained and entered a new phase by marriage with the new clan – that is the way life went on. The salmon and trout noticed no difference in the manner of fishing or the method used to cook them – there was safety in their numbers in those days.

The O'Cahans – O'Kanes eventually found themselves suffering the same fate as the O'Connors by the introduction of another clan, or rather race, the Plantation period under the local control of Sir Thomas Phillips. The changes of tenants in the Roe Valley over the centuries did not infringe upon the salmon and trout on their annual visitation to their spawning beds. A few gallons of human blood, now and then, over the years were an added vitamin to the fresh cool waters of the Roe. In what seems to be a pattern of each new race to claim supremacy over the Roe Valley, perhaps the next fifty to one-hundred years shall see a new guardian that will respect the river.

Time after time I have wandered along the banks of the Roe, not only to paint but also simply to enjoy the tranquillity and return to nature. I hope you will find the opportunity to take a stroll and find the magic that is abundant there.

The Glenshane.

This poem was by James O'Kane, known as the " Bard of Carntogher. " He was born in Swateragh in 1832 and died in 1913.

The Banks of the Roe

Dungiven, when darkness and silence surround you,
Enfolding your mountains that rise by the Roe,
I Think of the glories that covered and crowned you,
Your power and your splendour in days long ago.

Not far from your walls knelt the haughty Milesians,
Adoring their idols with pomp and with pride,
And here came the Druids, the Priests of the heathens,
To worship their gods on the green riverside.

But holy Saint Patrick the soil consecrated,
And preached the true Gospel to high and to low,
The vile works of Satan defied and defeated,
And planted the Cross on the Banks of the Roe!

Here stood the strong castle and halls of O'Cahan,
Here spread the broad acres held under his sway,
Beyond the Moyola the Bann and the Faughan,

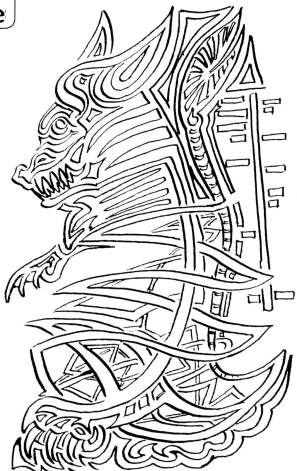

And here lies the dust of their Chieftain to-day!
Yes, here does he rest in your old church, Dungiven,
Who often in battle defeated the foe,
Unfurled Erin's flag to the free winds of Heaven,
And marshalled his troops on the banks of the Roe.

But, alas! By the Normans and Saxon invaders,
His halls and his castles were all levelled low,
The land was spoiled 'neath the rule of the raiders,
And freedom dethroned on the banks of the Roe!

The stranger may wonder that sweetness and sadness,
Entwine in our music and blend in our song,
And rightly conclude that this old land of gladness,
Has oft been oppressed by injustice and wrong.

The harp soon was silenced, the minstrel was banished,
Our mountain and valleys were held by the foe,
The last ray of freedom from Ulster had vanished,
And tyranny reigned on the banks of the Roe!

The end of March and the start of the fishing season in 1949 encouraged the Limavady fishermen to form a new club to promote their interest. Advertisements were placed in the local papers inviting interested parties to attend a meeting in Limavady.

> Limavady and District Anglers' Association.
>
> A CORDIAL INVITATION is extended to all Anglers interested in the revival of this Association to attend a MEETING in the TOWN HALL, LIMAVADY, on THURSDAY 31st MARCH, At 8 P.M.

Another notice in the press on 9th April 1949 went:-

Limavady Anglers.

——————————

Anglers, representative of the Limavady and Dungiven districts, met in the Limavady Town Hall when it was unanimously decided to form an association to be known as " The Roe Angling Association ", to take the place of the North Derry Angling Association, which had fallen into abeyance. Group-Captain E. F. Turner, A. F. C. presided.

The following officer-bearers were appointed; President: - Mr. James Stevenson, D. L. Vice – Presidents: - Miss Shearman; Colonel F. S. N. Macrory, D. S. O., D. L.; Colonel C. R. McCausland, D. L.; Sir Henry Macdonald-Tyler, C. I. E., D. L.; Head Constable T. J. Gibson and Mr. S. Troy, Coleraine. Chairman: Group Captain Turner; Hon. Secretary: Colonel L. Emmerson; Hon. Treasurer: Mr. C. C. Connolly, M. P. S.; Committee: - James Houston, Robert Simpson, Samuel Harper, J. Young and W. O'Hanlon.

" THE ANGLERS CARD " - was produced to promote a thoughtful fisherman, its contents are :-

To all ANGLERS
on the Roe.

_____
_____

Please read
and pass on to another.

_____

You fish on this river through the courtesy of the riparian owners.

We appeal to your sense of sportsmanship to help us keep the river "open" and fit for sportsmen by observing the following simple rules: -

DO PLEASE---

1. Avoid breaking down fences, walking through crops, and leaving litter on the banks.
2. Keep MOVING.
3. Fish pools in turn, allowing the angler in front a clear 30 yards start and maintain that distance.

4. Give fly rods priority.
5. Place all fish under 7" GENTLY back in the water with a wet hand.

PLEASE DO NOT---

1. Over-fish a pool.
2. Return to the head of a pool after having fished it and "step in" before an angler approaching from the pool above.
3. Commence fishing half way down a stretch or pool when another angler has commenced at the head.
4. Fish back up a pool when another angler is approaching.
5. "Step in" in front of another angler who has risen a fish and is "resting" the pool, or is waiting favourable condition before commencing to fish.

_____

Please keep this card and pass it to anyone you think is in need of it.

Another letter to the press.......April 16th, 1949.

Letter to the Editor.

Roe Angling Association.

Sir,

May we appeal, through the medium of your paper, to all anglers who fish the River Roe, to join the newly re-constituted " Roe Anglers Association ".

The objects the association has in view are to establish good relations with the owners of the land bordering the river and assist in the maintenance of fences and stiles; to endeavour to improve fishing in various ways such as restocking, attention to the river bed, the removal of snags and possibly, to improve and increase the natural food supply by the planting of beneficial weeds in places where they will grow.

The Roe is free to all comers, subject of course to the goodwill of the owners of the banks of the river. All fishermen will get the benefit of the Association's activities and we, therefore, ask all to assist us by joining and co-operating in our efforts to respect the property of the owners of the land who so kindly allow us to use it.

Much of the work involved will be carried out by the members voluntarily but the expenses will still be considerable and must be met from Association funds. The subscription for ordinary members is five shilling (minimum) payable to the hon. Treasurer, and applications for membership may be made to him or the hon. Secretary.

Yours, on behalf of the Committee and members: -
James Stevenson, President; E. F. Turner, Chairman; C. C. Connolly, hon. Treasurer, Main Street, Limavady; C. L. Emmerson, hon. Secretary, Leeke, Limavady.

28th May 1949

" Active Limavady Association "

Considerable progress in improving fishing facilities on the River Roe was reported at the first general meeting of the members of the recently formed Roe Angling Association held in Limavady on Friday evening, and an appeal for more voluntary labour to expedite the completion of the work met with a ready response.

The President, Mr. James Stevenson, D. L., extended a cordial welcome to the members and briefly outlined the objects of the Association.

Group Captain E. F. Turner, A. F. C., Chairman, who presided, said they were trying to make the Roe a very good fisherman's river.

Mr. Cyril Connolly, hon. Treasurer. Reported that the membership now stood at 75, and the hon. Secretary, Colonel C. L. Emmerson, made various suggestions in regard to restocking and improving trout.

Other work was being carried out along the banks of the Roe at this time, from the junction of the Owenreagh with the Roe at Dungiven to Lough Foyle, not by the Anglers Association, but by the Ministry of Agriculture. Their work entailed repairs due to storm and flood damage and the Drainage Council were urged to repair the embankments to remove the threat of flooding to 3000 acres of rich fertile land.

Hugh Smith, who was born in Scotland, loved his new adopted home in Maine, as this poem shows and he was also a keen fisherman. He called his poem…..

Along the River Roe

One morning as I walked abroad,
With angling rod in hand,
When spring's life giving voice was heard.
Green verdure decked the land.
The little lambs in thoughtless glee,
Ran bounding to and fro,
On primrose banks that bloom so fair,
Along the river Roe.

The blackbird sang his mellow song,
Enchanting to the ear,
The mavis gave his lively notes,
In variations clear.
The wood-larks lofty strains aroused,
My thoughts of long ago,
And memory mused on childhood's days,
Along the river Roe.

As the feathered choir, both large and small,
Did dame Natures praise,
Her tears of dew like sparkling gems,
Refreshed those flower glad braes.
The daisies kissed the rising sun,
Like little stars below,
And a gleam from Eden seemed to shine,
Along the river Roe.

The trout and salmon do abound,
Along this stream so rare,
Where angling was my chief delight,
Oft-times my greatest care.
But fate, disguised in prospects garb,
Sent me afar to go,
And bid farewell to bygone scenes,
Along the river Roe.

I oft have trod the banks of Clyde,
Where wealth and honour shine,
Where science in advancing steps,
Towards perfection climbs.
Affection clings round that fair spot,
Where fossil babies grow,
Near to the well-known planting ford
Along the river Roe.

As you walk along that river side,
You'll see historic scenes,
A circling rampart called the Forth,
Once raised up by the Danes.
It was there they fought with sling and stone,
Or drew the archers bow,
But were forced to leave those peaceful homes,
Along the river Roe.

We are told of Egypt's pyramids,
And catacombs of Rome,
Though old, they're but the works of men,
We've better far at home.
The Carrick owns a structure grand,
But nature made it so,
Where her special handy works are seen,
Along the river Roe.

The king of poets praised the Doon,
Likewise the banks o' Ayr,
And others praised the lovely Clyde,
And Kelvin's winding fair.
But had these poets seen the land,
Where shamrocks love to grow,
Where the charms of nature are complete,
Along the river Roe.

Hugh Smith put his name forward as a candidate for the Limavady Rural District Council for Lislane in 1899.

Colonel C. L. Emmerson was the Honourable Secretary of the Roe Anglers Association in its early days and the following is his synopses of the river Roe as an advertising vehicle.

" FISHING ON THE ROE " (Date 1955)

"The river Roe, from the anglers point of view, is mainly interesting on account of the runs of salmon and sea trout which commence, as a rule, towards the middle of the summer and continues to the end of the season on the 20th October. It also contains large numbers of game, small brown trout. There are no course fish except eels. As the river is 'spate-fed', salmon and sea trout fishing is only worthwhile after a 'fresh' has come down, but brown trout fishing, which commences on April 1st, is practicable at most times except during a prolonged drought.

The river rises in the Glenshane Pass and after a rapid descent through Dungiven to Limavady flattens out somewhat and enters Lough Foyle 30 miles from its source. The bed of the river varies between rock and sand or shingle, the latter predominating in the flatter stretches. There is no mud. It is mostly wadeable and many portions can, to advantage, only be fished in this way. The bottom is firm and safe with practically no potholes.

Free access is allowed at present, by the owners, to the banks throughout most of its course. Exceptions are as follows: -

PELLIPAR DEMESNE: Permission must be obtained from the Land Stewart.
ELECTRICITY BOARD PROPERTY: This includes most of the right bank between Roe Mill Weir and Roe Mill and the banks of the mill streams supplying the power station. Permits, on payment of 5/-(25p today), can be obtained from the office of the E.B.N.I. in Linenhall Street, Limavady.

ROE PARK: Permits on payment of 5/- will be obtained from "The Farm Office", Roe Park.
BELLARENA DEMESNE: Angling forbidden.

LICENCES: A licence is necessary in order to fish for salmon and sea trout. The cost is 40/- (£2.today) and licences can be obtained from Mr. C. C. Connolly, 38 Main Street, Limavady. A licence issued in other fishery districts in Northern Ireland is valid on procuring a supplementary salmon licence, price 10/-(50p today), from Mr. Connolly. No licence is required for brown trout angling in the Londonderry district (which does not include the rivers in the East side of the county).

ROE ANGLING ASSOCIATION: The association exists to maintain and improve angling on the Roe. Members enjoy the privilege of fishing in Pellipar, and the other preserved portions mentioned above without further payment.

VISITORS who intend to fish are advised to join as temporary members. Application should be made to the Hon. Treasurer, Mr. C. C. Connolly, from whom particulars can be obtained. A very useful fishing guide with a sketch plan and brief description of salmon pools is on sale to members.

This was the advertised information placed with the Limavady Official Guide, 1955.

The following pages contain some of Cyril Connolly's notes, with the consent of Mrs. Connolly.

——————————— ROE ANGLER NOTES. ———————————

April 1950 - Col. Emmerson and C. C. Connolly collected 10,000 fry from Hyde Park Hatchery and sowed same in Gelvin, Drenagh, Owenbeg and Killyblaught.

April - Col. Emmerson and M. Mcpherson sowed 5,000 Bann Fry (salmon) at Owenbeg.

May - Amy and Cyril - lost 15 trout above bridge to Red Spinner - cause - missing barb.

May - Outing of 42 members. Hardy 1st. with two trout 10 ½ ozs. Rankin 2nd. Hutten 3rd.

June - Amy - one to Badger Quill. Got fire brigade to pump out trapped water at Asken Pool to release Fry - about 70 rescued.

June - Saw good take of sea trout and occasional salmon by nets - Haygates.

——————————————

March 1952 - Month came in mild and everything seemed to progress rapidly - birds were early. Towards the later end of the month the weather got hard and cold with East wind predominating. A very poor season - no water - the nets did very well

——————————————

August 1953 - August Flax water killed upwards of 100 salmon in Givens Pool - McCallion and Cyril helped save 20 whilst members of Kingfishers Club filled their bags.

October - Went to Flat (Carrick) and waded out halfway - brought 2 fish to feet twice. Reminded me of a dog playing with a ball. Amy came in when I moved up and she killed the fish. I had another offer from behind stone. Amy came up and killed this one too. McCollum gaffed both for her.

——————————————

I suppose no man likes to admit it, but Cyril could.......The lady could fish and kill.

The Birren Bridge is draped on all sides with trees and shrubbery to such a degree that you drive over it without realising you have crossed the river. The area is secluded in the townland of Cluntygeeragh, *cluainte-geaorach, the meadows of the sheep,* and to the north overlooked by the Boviel, *both-Mhicil, the hut of Michael.*

The salmon, when looking for spawning beds, feel the cooler change in the water temperature as they swim around the boulders that litter the river beds up here in the Glenshane. The water sparkles when the sunlight glints through the hazel and elder trees that grace the banks of the river carpeted in rich mosses. The risk of pollution, up here in the high glens, is very minimal but heavy rain can wash a dense mixture of black water from the heather clad bog terrain surrounding the river.

The ford in this painting is called Crabarkey, *Cro-Bairche, the enclosure for cattle*, or *Bairches fold.* It is one of the few remaining fords left on the river. However during heavy rainstorms the water level rises considerably here and it is impossible to drive a car over. The pedestrian has the advantage by using the foot-bridge and can stop to enjoy the view, both up and down the river, from the height and central location where he stands.

This basin is surrounded by a natural rath, that contributes to the name of the townland, in the secluded glen of Benady.

Again the riverbed is strewn with boulders that throw the water in spasms, this way and that, creating a healthy energy that encourages the fish along. Reeds, hazel, willow, birch and beech trees line the banks and these determine the expertise of the angler with the fly among the calm, singing water of the Roe.

April 1954 - First lot of salmon fry delivered from Newtownstewart Hatchery sown in the Gelvin and Killyblaught.

Collected second batch of fry from Newtownstewart Hatchery - one showed casualties at Dungiven Bridge and we (S. Harper, W. McCallion, Amy and Allen) hastily dumped same into the river below the Bridge - rest were sown without loss.

May - Freshets nearly every day in the Roe for the past week. Got agreement and cases signed by the farmers – Cyril, L. Brown, S. Harper, Amy and W. Hardy.

July - the nets had a bumper week.

August - 600 fish killed in the nets this Week.

September - fished the Springs and Carrick Flat – connected with fish opposite 'big rock' and broke my rod in landing the fish.

September - gaffed fish for Rev. McCully, his first in run above the Curly burn.

The 1954 fishing season had ended with certain achievements by the Roe Anglers Association and as the angler knows it required a steady pressure. Our Annual General Meeting was held on 5th March - we pressed hard at the meeting to get control of the river and finally succeeded in having the stretch from the Burnfoot Bridge to Bellarena Bridge land from the farmers. Got signboards erected and had some trouble from the locals who tore down several of them.

The following proposals were carried unanimously by the Advisory Council - To prohibit spinning after 15th April. To Prohibit Bamboo Rods greater than ¾ " at Butt. And night fishing after 31st August.

At the end of March 1955 there was a meeting in Lifford of the Foyle Advisory Board to discuss new regulations pertaining to the River Roe and Fahan. After long arguments we got the Commission to waive rule 2 - Prohibition of bait fishing. The Reverend Smyth - a nasty piece of work, and I would not trust him in sight of a spent fish - Minister - an old nuisance - all out for themselves. Pretty bad with the flue and glad to get home!
April - sowed 35,000 fry in river Roe at Roe Park.

At the Annual General Meeting, held in the Alexander Town Hall, on the 2nd March 1956, George H. Tyler was elected President.
The Previous President of the Roe Anglers Association, Mr James Stevenson, died on 16th July 1956.

March 1957 - Meeting in Town Hall to expel W.....H...... for snatching - failure due to packed meeting.
The annual General Meeting was held on 11th March.
12th March - Percy Quinn gave a demonstration on fly tying in Cyril Connolly's home.
April 1957 - 10,000 fry put in by Dungiven Anglers.

September 1957 - Gaffed fish for Speedy Moore in Brittains Wrack in shallow water - never again as fish ran between my legs - always gaff deep!

8th June 1959 - 130 sea trout caught by McCurry's net - Smaller in size than usual.
For the Anglers the possibility of removing all nets from the Roe was a problem greater then the Mccurrys.

July 1966 - Bright morning - did not fish - hottest day of the year. Amy arrived at 11 a.m. - sunbathed after catching a fish. Tried the Carrick stream without response. Cloudy around 8p.m. John arrived and we fished till 10p.m. without offers. Fished Mill stream. Gave John fish to divide with Herbie McIlwaine.
August 1967 - Rang Billy Moody and gave him permission to fish. Just had about all I could take in the shop and was glad to reach the river at 8 p.m. Billy had just finished killing 4 fish - 2 at the Meetings - 1 at Pot and 1 at the Carrick Rock to No.8 Shrimp - similar to Hot Orange - must get the dressing. 8.45 p.m. got on the water and rose two in the Pot, then got into one and lost it. Lost another in Mill Stream and another at Carrick Rock - all to No.8 R.S. and No.6 Hot Orange Shrimp - Carbuncle marks on two of Billy's fish - on nose and tail. They look nothing like my fish, which I had on earlier. - Not a fresh run! I am afraid disease is beginning.

SALMO TRUTTA

Or as we simply call it " Brown Trout " is a freshwater fish, prefering the burns and small streams as their home. He is a territorialist and spends a large part of its time chasing intruders from its domain - they are not gergarious. Brown trout in the small burns that feed the river Roe never exceed a few ounces in weight, and are comfortable in the cooler waters of these mountain streams. Those that live in the river migrate into streams and burns such as the Curly, castle, Gelvin, Owenbeg, etc. to breed. Favourable conditions may generate from the end of September as the trout wait for natures signal to find a spawning bed in flowing water - not still water.

The sporting angler usually uses a catch and release attitude, using a barbless hook, when he plays a small brown trout to the bank. The fish must be carefully released using hands that have been cooled under the water as the normal temperature of the hand can burn the fish. The experience of being hooked, handled and released is very traumatic to the fish.

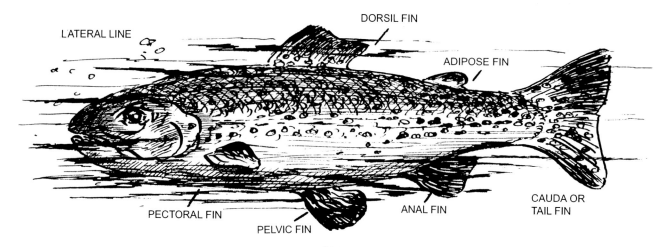

LATERAL LINE

DORSIL FIN

ADIPOSE FIN

PECTORAL FIN

PELVIC FIN

ANAL FIN

CAUDA OR
TAIL FIN

A 1906 poem from a Dungiven man :-

The Bonnie Roe Water sae close tae my Hame

The Bann an' the Shannon, the Liffy, the Dee,
The sparklin' Blackwater, the sweet river Lee,
Ye've a' heard their praises, in storie or rame,
But the bonnie Roe water lies close tae my hame.

Then why should I no some merit discover,
In thy glitterin' green glades, the resort o' lovers,
Thy pools an' thy shallows my possy maun claim,
For the bonnie Roe water lies close tae my hame.

The rock o' O' Kaghan, its chieftain lies sleepin,
In the deep swirlin' pool, consigned to the
    keepin',
'Tis the angels "reville" shall summon O'Kane,
From the bonnie Roe waters sae close tae my
    Hame.

The Dog-Leap renowned, how aft did I stray,
Neath shelterin' shade an' caught white spray,
As it turned in the alleys o' black slaty stane,
The bonnie Roe water sae close tae my hame.

The slopes o' the Largy, sweet Templemoyle,
Has held the white linen, a glitterin' coil,
Unrivalled for bleachin', noo only the name,
The bonnie Roe water sae close tae my hame.

How aft hae we pondered in tent or in barrick
The misapplied lessons we learned in the
    Carrick,
But our gaze is more holy as it rests on that
    Fame,
On the bonnie Roe waters sae close tae my
    Hame.

Ye braes o' Devenny, yer broon nut an' sloe,
Tempted the schuleboys o' Aiken a nuttin' tae go,
Aft crossed Ligaliree their treasures tae claim,
On the bonnie Roe waters sae close tae my hame.

The Burnfit an' Boiley, the circle horse shoe
Her charms an' her beauties, ivery wind that hes blew,
An' ruffed the eddies as it corrsed tae the main,
O, the bonnie Roe water sae close tae my hame.

Then here's tae each fond heart that's noo ower the ocin,
When ye mention Roe water their heart's sweet emotion,
Beats time tae their thoughts as they follow the train,
O' the bonnie Roe water sae close tae my hame.

_____

The Carnick Weir.

In the extreme weather conditions of winter the clothing that offered most protection and retained the warmth of the body was leather. It was natural that the residents around the hills of Benbradagh would adopt the animal skin not only for clothing but also the name of their territory - Dungiven, *Dun-Gaimhean, the fortress of the skins.*

Turmeel, *tur-maol, the Derelict Tower,* it is to this area that the last wolf in the county sought refuge when chased out of Magilligan three centuries ago.

The Plantation period dispersed all the old clan tradition but many years after the O'Cahan chiefs disappeared a plaintive bard still offered their praise: -

"From Elaghs Throne in
     Ennishowen,
O'Dougherty came shouting;
From Kennaughts plain came
     Manus Kane,
A victory not doubting".

This painting was accomplished from the bank of a fishing pool called *Tubba-na-Cush* or more commonly Whinney Island, in the townland of Derryard, *Doire-Ard, the high oak grove.*

The culmination of three or four townlands at one location, to my mind, tend to represent a meeting of old friends, which is the case here. The townlands which are visible from Derryard are Scriggan, *Creagan, The Stony Ground;* Derryware, *Doire-mhaor, the Oakgrove of The Stewards,* and Lackagh, *Leacach, abounding in flagstones.*

Pellipar House stands in Lackagh townland and the out-buildings of the farm acknowledge the utilisation of the flagstones in their rustic setting. Old Benbradagh, in stern consternation, stands close by over-looking this meadow, with Donalds Hill and Benevenagh in the distance.

The ladies need not be forgotten for their love of the river Roe, either when walking or fishing, as is evident in this 1899 poem written by a lady who lived in the Dungiven area.

A Day in Leafy June

I remember a day in leafy June,
When we walked in the woods together,
And green were the fields and the land lay fair,
In the glow of golden weather.

The wild rose peeped from the thorny bank,
And the lark from the scented clover,
Sprang into the air with a glad refrain,
Like the song of a happy lover.

The ferns by the wayside bent their heads,
To the south wind gently wooing,
And down in the glen where the oak trees grow,
We could hear the wood-dove cooing.

And the song of the thrush was a burst of joy,
That came from the hazel cover,
To his mate where she sat in the sheltered nest
In the woods of green Altmover.

Now chilling winds with a wailing moan,
Are taking the leaves away,
And day by day the flowers die,
With a gradual sad decay.

Ah, me, how soon is glory gone,
And the woodland music's still,
And nature's voice is nearly hushed,
And the song of the sunlit rill.

But the day of the rose month's perfect grace,
With joy I shall remember,
When the birds are mute and the roses fled,
And chill blows bleak December.

Still I'll hear the breeze through the trees,
See the blue sky bending over,
And my thoughts go back to the morning fair,
In the woods of green Altmover.

fly Tying

An art and craft that emulates natures' menu on offer to the salmon and trout, it requires an observant, articulated person to accomplish the finished enticement to deploy.

Cyril Connolly took notes and enquired from other anglers about this quill or that hackle, or the variety of ribbing threads used. A list for the winter season is a program most anglers have set themselves to tie - One of Cyril's was "The Greenwell" – the material, colours and techniques to use. To develop into a "master fly tier" requires more than one season of experience, some of the old hands will still admit "there's a lot to learn yet". Patience is a virtue that all anglers are born with.

These are a few of Cyril's notes on fly tying. The notes are not fully explanatory; therefore it would be advisable for the novice fly tier to consult the aid of an experienced angler.

TINSEL BODIES.

Tie ribbing underneath body and push to lift. The tinsel for the body is now cut off and the usual diagonal cut made across the end of it. Place underneath the body with the cut edge of tinsel at right angles to the hook. Tie in, with one twine of silk, made to hold it in position. The extreme cut end is then curled up and over the body and two very tight twines of silk made to hold it in position. A piece of flux silk is tied in at the shoulder and wound down to tinsel and back again. One complete twine of the tinsel is now taken over the body – covering the point of the cut end of the tinsel. The diagonal is still apparent and the next twine of tinsel must follow this wire. Each twine must lie edge to edge and pull tight. When shoulder is reached two twines of silk are put round the tinsel and the surplus broken off --back to the rib. Make one complete twine round extreme edge and tie tinsel in tight over spirals anti-clockwise to shoulder. Tie underneath shank and varnish.

TUBE FLIES.

Tube on tapered salmon hook eyeless – size to suit tube and firm enough to hold if from rotating easily. Bend to hook placed in vice. Tying silk run down tube and body silk of tinsel and rib – tied on at what would be the tail of the normal fly. Wind it to the front and follow with body to form a bed for the ends of the hair fibres. Best fibres of hair usually found at base of tail. Hairs are cut from springs by twisting a small bunch of them together and cutting off as near to root as possible. Fur at base of fibres combed out with point of dubbing needle. A small quantity used at one time – approx. 1/16th when twisted together. First bunch is then tied on top of tube as method for feather wings. Waste ends cut off. Do this after each bunch is tied in. Second bunch is tied in immediately to right of first bunch after rotating the tube. Carry on until complete circumference of tube is covered. A single lap of silk is then taken round all the fibres up to where the first bunch was tied in.

Whip finish - and one or two coats of alum soaked well into silk whippings. When dry add a final coat of black or red varnish.

Hackle - This may be added - tied in front at the same point where first bunch was tied in.

"HACKLES".

Draw through the fingers so that the fibres stand out at right angles to stem. Tie in at eye with stem at right angles to the hook shank and fibres perpendicular to hook shank. Tip pointing away from tier.

Wind silk in tight even twines back to body tying in the stem of the hackle which has been bent back. Wind the hackle tip to the body keeping it tight. Tie in the tip and continue winding silk through the hackle to the eye of the hook. Then two twines in front of the first fibre - whip finish.

Doubling - hackle tied by butt or tip to hook and held vertically by the hackle pliers, The fibres are then stroked to the aft.

Stiffening "dry fly hackle" - select a large hackle of same colour and cut off about 1" from tip. Stroke fibres to right angles and clip to $1/8^{th}$" either side of stem length of fibres according to size of fly. The hackle is now tied into the shoulder of fly and one or two twines made before tying off. The effective hackle is then tied in and wound behind and in front of cut hackle.

Water proofing hackles - dilute varnish and coat fibres to right angle with varnish moistened fingers - bulldog clip to dry same.

Pellipar House, Dunsiven

33

A Dungiven man expressed his feelings, in 1906, for his local mountain and called his poem......

Benbrada

(Benbradagh)

I have seen thee, sweet Benbrada,
When the gentle voice o' spring,
Brocht lambkins tae thy bosom,
And garred the birdies sing.
An led thy sides wi daisies,
And wi violets vernal bloom,
Made yer feet a blazin' Eden,
With the boony bush o' broom.

I have seen thee' sweet Benbrada,
When the bonnie summer sun,
Went chasin' ower the heather,
It's dancin' beamlets rin.
Reflected like a mirror,
When wanderin' thro' the dell,
It struck thy glessy bosom,
O' thy modest stream, Strone Gell.

I have seen thee, sweet Benbrada,
When the hunters ringin' shot,
Foretauld the death o' pheasant,
Wild pigeon, or moorcock.
When yer stately spruce an' noble fir,
Was clothed in belts o' cones,
An' autumn mourned departed days,
With plaintive, wearie moans.

I have seen thee, sweet Benbrada,
When winter's snowy white,
Ower thy lofty head an shoulders,
Cast her robes o' spotless bright.
When glitterin' frosty diamonds,
Forged yer gemy sparklin' crown,
An not a sign o' life but me,
Could on yer form be found.

I have seen thee, sweet Benbrada,
When the cloudland did descend,
An heaven, with misty shroudlings,
Hid each rocky curve and bend.
An revealed yer form an figure,
Cled wi silver threads o' dew,
When the aist leams o'er the mornin',
All the shadows frae thee drew.

I have seen night's shadows lengthenin',
Ower thee throw its inky pall,
Dumbstruck, the voice of nature,
Held in its mystic thrall.
When bats an' owlets dared,
To scan thy rugged face,
An' the tremblin' rabbit, grown bold,
Runs in the wanton race.

I have seen thee, sweet Benbrada,
When the storm kings ower thee rode,
When wirlwinds built their castles,
An' the tempest claimed abode.

When heaven's artillery thunderin',
Ye re-echoed once again,
An lightnin's fiery courser charged,
Ower the Scriggan plain.

I love thee, sweet Benbrada,
Iviry bush an ivery stane,
Iviry sloe on Tannerafie,
Iviry flower on Curragh's plain.
My fandest wish, when death's rap comes,
An this warrin' spirit's fled,
Is tae sleep in the inner circle,
'neath the stanes o' Cranu's bed.

I have seen the laftiest mountains,
In al' this world's domain,
Sky-cleavin' giants risen frae,
India's burnin' plain,
Terrific, grand, majestic,
But still it wasna hame,
It is that robes Benbrada,
Wi' a glamour a' its ain.

With the formation of the new Roe Anglers Association there was a need to furnish a bank account with necessary funds to accomplish the future tasks thought beneficial to the Roe. The first venture was a concert. The venue was held in the Alexander Town Hall an the 5th December 1949 and the Chairman, Group Captain E. F. Turner, gave a homely welcome to the artists from Derry City. For the Londonderry Male Singers, with Mrs. I. H. Wilson as their conductor, there was an air of excitement as they entered the hall. From solo pieces to a well-rehearsed choral selection of songs, the choir were applauded as a well drilled body with a pleasing tone. Mr. William Wood, Mr. William Loughlin and Mr. Wilson Hamilton performed the solo parts.

Mr. Gordon Douglas, who accompanied himself with the accordion, was a "big hit" which was evident due to the "encore". His pleasing stage manner had the audience completely captivated with his delightful singing and intimate style. The concert lasted three hours with a high standard of music. The soloists proved their adept talents without question - the best. They were Miss Lyle Acheson, Miss Margaret Hamilton and the gentlemen already mentioned. The virtuoso effort on the violin by Bobbie Bell sent ripples through the angler's hands. Flight-Lieut. Lloyd performed amusing impressions to diversify the long show. The local highlight, and one of the most interesting features of the evening, was an illusionist act contributed by Cyril Connolly of Limavady. Scots songs in the "Will Fyffe" manner by Jock Gilmour also contributed to a grand evening of entertainment. Mr Jack Taggart and Mrs. Wilson provided the accompaniments.

To wind up the enjoyable evening Group Captain Turner expressed his sincere thanks on behalf of the Anglers and played host, along with other club members, by providing a grand supper for the entertainers.

After all the expenses for the performers, the supper, etc. the Roe Anglers ended the evening with a profit of £19.16.02 and their fund was well under way.

Benbradagh stands towering 1535 feet above sea level, overlooking the Roe Valley and the glens of Benedy and Owenreagh, that were glacially gorged by unimaginable time, never mind the size of the ice sheets. Over the gradual rising hills and down the glens once rode the lord of the Isle – " the O'Neil ", friend of the O'Cahans, expecting and receiving the honour due to a master. As did the O.Cahans expect and receive the tithes of their lesser subjects in the Roe Valley. Granie Roe - the banshee who encumbered the O'Cahans still cries at the homes about to receive an unwelcome event.

" In the lands of O'Cahans where bleak mountains rise, o'er whose brown ridgy tops now the dusky cloud flies. Deep sunk in a valley a wild flower did grow and her name was Finvola -

The gem of the Roe. "

The slope of the hill, Largy, *Leargaidh*, drops very sharply as it reaches and braces the river Roe on the east bank. In this painting, which I call Sam Connors Corner, the rock face of the Carrick suddenly ceases and the green fields, edged with hawthorn, bracken and winns, take their place. The area is full of contrasting rock formations, gravel beds, heavy boulder clay banks and grass walks, encased with mature beech, elm and willow trees. There is so much to observe that a day with a flask and sandwiches could be spent, seated now and then, absorbing the beauty. It is an intriguing spot for the angler as well I might add.

The west bank of the river is in the parish of Balteagh, *Both-Dha-Fhiach,* and the townlands of Terrydremont, both north and south, sympathetically guide the Roe on further.

The life of a salmon.

From early July Salmon have a natural instinct to reach a spawning bed. On a gravel or sandy bed, within the shallows at the source of the river, a hen salmon deposits something like 7,000 eggs in one *redd* – this is a recess created by the hen and cock fish to retain their off spring. This process is repeated at various locations, perhaps not far away from each other, 3 or 4 times as assurance that some of the eggs will survive the possibility of attack by disease or predators. They cover the *redd* with sand and gravel after the eggs have been fertilised.

From the end of August onwards fish have a destiny, and the final curtain is drawn upon these *kelts*, as they are known after their supreme effort to give life to their species. These *kelts*, weak and spent, die looking as though time took a surge and aged them because of this natural cycle. Slow death transpires as they swim down river deflated and easy prey to all scavengers – that is the culmination of their beauty.

By mid winter the eggs, *ova*, are about ready to hatch, the general cycle is about three months. When the young, known as *alevin*, burst forth nature has provided them with a sack of food attached under their throat. Five weeks later the *alevin* have developed their own feeding habits – the sack of food is empty and they are now called *fry* – at one inch in length.

Over a two-year period the fry stay in the river and gorge themselves. They are now known as *parr*. Like the ugly duckling their scales change colour and the energy they display in jumping about the stream resembles the spring lambs. They are now called *smolt*. They look like salmon now, silver and sleek, on their journey down river to the sea and the north Atlantic.

In time they return to the home of their birth. If they weigh around seven pounds they are known as *grilse*, any bigger and they are salmon. They now swim up the river and the process starts all over again.

The Burnfoot BRIDGE.

A few more notes on fly tying - From Cyril Connolly's diary.

" WINGS "

Form loop and pull down - then make three twines to right of loop silk. Form loop - bring silk under and up before pulling upwards to tighten. Do not pull the silk tighter after removing the fingers.

Using pliers ---- pass at least two twines of tying silk through the eye of the tool, then hold the tool by the jaws that grip the wing - (not too tight) -, pull silk then. Put another twine of silk around the hook shank before removing the pliers.

Upright Wings ---- two twines around the base, then one around the shank – figure eight here between them to make them separated.

Wings forward in Dry Fly ----- wings are tied in before body and tail. Wind hackle at back of wing – practice with " mallard primary quill ". For softer materials use double slips.

Using Loop of Fine Wire ----- loop over feathers to be tied in – pull down – then push ends of wire to left before tying with silk.

Teal Mallard ---- cut a left and right hand strip leaving the quill on. Straighten out the fibres to stand at right angles to the quills – then place one on top of the other – best side down. Now cut the quills off both strips and fold exactly in half – a small "V" cut midway in both feathers helps this.

Any river that sports fish cannot escape the attention of the poacher; the Roe is no exception.

Limavady Petty Sessions Oct. 13th 1906 (fishing)

Sir Thomas Lecky presiding.

James Loughery, of Carrick, summoned by John Kerr, a water bailiff, for alleged " beating " the water of the Roe at Carrick - to drive fish to bank.

Mr. G. E. Proctor solicitor for Conservators of Fisheries.
Mr. Wm. Horner for Loughery, the defendant.

John Kerr stated that, about ten o'clock on the morning of the 29th Sept., he was walking along checking the portion of the river at the Carrick. He noticed Loughery kneeling down, shading his brow with his cap, and looking into the river. Loughery was then observed wading in around the rocks in the centre of the river, poking with a stick round the rocks. Kerr believed Loughery was trying to drive the fish to the brew. Kerr then approached Loughery, who noticed him and ran off into the hazel bushes on the other side. Kerr managed to question Loughery, who said he was not looking for fish - 'they were scarce anyway' he said.
Loughery was fined £2.

Hugh Smith, from Maine, continued with his verses of praise for the area, and in 1900 he was taking a cool look at the Gelvin Burn. The Gelvin joins the river Roe in the parish of Bovevagh.

The Gelvin Burn

Give Erin yet another bard,
With gifted pen and voice to praise,
Her variegated landscapes,
Her flowery glens and fertile braes.
Her towering hills and winding rills,
Benbradagh, Gelvin and the Roe,
Where Erins grandeurs yet are fresh,
To-day as long ago.

We love those haunts of childhood,
As something sacred and sublime,
Engraved on our memory,
Unblotted by the hand of time.
For youthful scenes, like golden dreams,
To fancy vision oft return,
That's why I chant the praises,
Of the banks and braes of Gelvin Burn.

In the dawning of life's morning,
I've often strayed its banks along,
Charmed by the sweetly smiling flowers,
The dancing stream and warblers song.
While 'mong the trees the scented breeze,
Did softly breathe times fleeting sigh,
And bowed the willows silken bloom,
To kiss the stream that glided by.

Fair and pure as Edens bowers,
Flourish thorns of spotless white,
And send their fragrant odours far,
Beneath meridian beams most bright.
Enraptured, I thus fondly mused,
Why "man was never made to mourn",
I rather praised the Hand Divine,
That formed the banks of Gelvin Burn.

As nature's fairy fountain,
It sparkles down the mountain's brow,
And splashing as it onward plays,
Round many a rustic knowe.
Where woodbine climbs and gently twines,
Around the thorn that bears the sloe,
And blends its pleasant fragrance,
With thyme that there in wildness grow.

Benbradagh, old and hoary,
Still smiles down on the lowland soil,
That paradise of Erin, dressed,
By the honest sons of toil.
May blessings come to every home,
Rejoicing all that there sojourn,
While fortune smiles, like nature on,
The banks and Braes of Gelvin Burn.

———————————

WARBLER.

On the Largy braes, central in this painting, there still stands Sam Connors old home. Sam, who was known as the Largy poet, emigrated to Canada in 1925, and we know from his poems that he could not find another Largy in Brampton, Ontario.

The river makes a sharp turn at this point and sturdy rock braces prevent the destruction of the Largy braes. As you can see from the rock strewn foreground the river is a determined fellow who dismantled the manmade weir in the centre.

" A Fisherman's Prayer. "
God grant that I may live,
To fish until my dying day,
And when it comes to my
    last cast,
I then most humbly pray,
That I may be allowed to
    stray,
In summer, along the
    Largy Brae.

The view around the Carrick valley from Ballymully, *Baile – Mullaigh, the townland of the summit,* offers an expanse of landscape so impressive. How the ice flow, thousands of years ago, carved out this valley and deposited the bolder clay in seemingly random design to produce our Vale of the Roe is beyond imagination.

North and south Terrydremont townlands *Tir-ui-Dhromain, O'Drummond's district* and *Tir-a-Druimin, the land of the little ridge,* are located on the right of the painting descending to the banks of the Roe. The descent is not all gradual, an abrupt ridge of rocks line the river for a few hundred yards and the only path to the water is via the church grounds. Take this walk slowly and the iron bridge at the bottom offers some amazing views and the prospect of the other bank to ascend, draped in wild flowers.

BRIDGE AT THE CARRICK.

Map 1 from Dungiven to the Green Bridge.

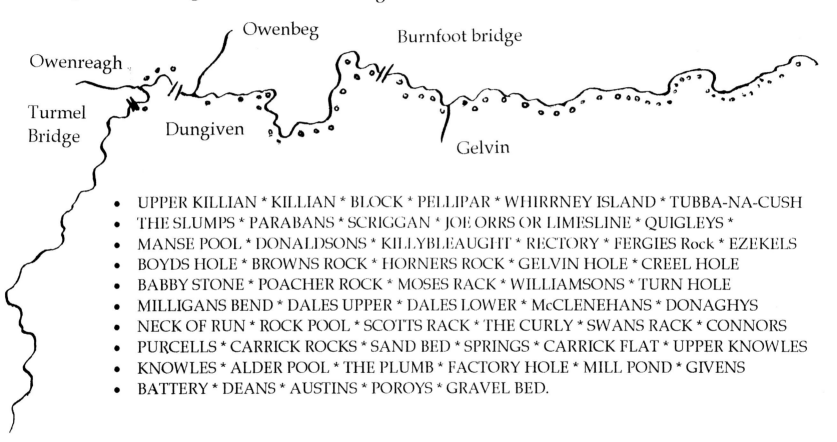

Owenbeg

Burnfoot bridge

Owenreagh

Turmel Bridge

Dungiven

Gelvin

- UPPER KILLIAN * KILLIAN * BLOCK * PELLIPAR * WHIRRNEY ISLAND * TUBBA-NA-CUSH
- THE SLUMPS * PARABANS * SCRIGGAN * JOE ORRS OR LIMESLINE * QUIGLEYS *
- MANSE POOL * DONALDSONS * KILLYBLEAUGHT * RECTORY * FERGIES Rock * EZEKELS
- BOYDS HOLE * BROWNS ROCK * HORNERS ROCK * GELVIN HOLE * CREEL HOLE
- BABBY STONE * POACHER ROCK * MOSES RACK * WILLIAMSONS * TURN HOLE
- MILLIGANS BEND * DALES UPPER * DALES LOWER * McCLENEHANS * DONAGHYS
- NECK OF RUN * ROCK POOL * SCOTTS RACK * THE CURLY * SWANS RACK * CONNORS
- PURCELLS * CARRICK ROCKS * SAND BED * SPRINGS * CARRICK FLAT * UPPER KNOWLES
- KNOWLES * ALDER POOL * THE PLUMB * FACTORY HOLE * MILL POND * GIVENS
- BATTERY * DEANS * AUSTINS * POROYS * GRAVEL BED.

The joy that this young poetess felt was evidently twofold. Everything about the Carrick Rocks, near where she lived, reflected her own passion for the subject of her desire, I'm afraid I know not whom. In 1880, when she wrote this poem, I am sure he would be well aware of how she felt for him.

The Song of the Bird

The WREN.

"I love you, I love you", I heard the bird sing,
'Twas a lark that sprang up with the dew on it's wing,
"Sweetheart, I love you the summer day long",
I sing in my heart as the bird sings its song.

Then a thrush in the holly caught up the same strain,
And poured out his heart in the gladsome refrain,
And the song that he sang from dawn till grey,
Was "sweetheart, I'll love you a year and a day".

The stream rippled softly the willows among,
And I knew by its murmur, it sang the same song,
And all the sweet wildflowers shook lightly to say,
"Dear-heart, we love you as long as we may".

But a brown little robin, half hid in the leaves,
Says, "he who sings sweetest most surely deceives,
When summer is over and winter winds roar,
Dear-heart, you will find then their loving times o'er.

But I'll not forsake thee when hushed is the song,
I'll gladden your heart all the dark winter long,
Through sunshine or shadow be skies blue or grey,
Dear-heart, I'll love you for ever and aye ".

Then all the birds joined in the robins' sweet song,
All the streamlets chimed in as it glided along,
And the song they all sang at the close of the day,
Was," Dear-heart, I love you for ever and aye ".

The Mavis

The Roe Anglers Association made efforts to restock the river with fry. A hard working member, Mr Samuel McCorkill, was regularly observed collecting containers to transport the fry to advantageous locations.
In 1956 Sam McCorkill, Cyril Connolly, William Hardy and P. Quinn sowed 100,000 salmon fry at Roe Park, Derrybeg bridge, Bolea bridge (The Curly Burn), and in the Castle Burn at Drummond. The Bann fry (salmon) were selected as a sturdy stock for the Roe that same year.

The old Ford at the Carrick Mills is a favourite area for the visitor, as well as the angler, because the convenient car park offers a central location from which to take advantage of the walks and the footbridge that leads over the river to other paths. The old lanes on either side of the river guide you to the ford and the rock foundation is very evident under the cascades of the water. It is used occasionally by a farmer with a tractor. The industry that once thrived here is gone – the extinguished flax trade though has left a few sad relicts – the dilapidated sheds.

The river here is still in the company of Terrydremont and Largy townlands. Keep your eyes alert for a little feathered fisherman, a patient little fellow sitting on a rock, moving occasionally up and down the river, as the Roe intrigues his dinner along – he is of course the heron.

I could not leave the Carrick Flats without trying to display the simplicity and tranquillity of the braes and foliage, and thankfully the absence of industry. This point of the river is still in the townlands of Largy and Terrydremont, and our little feathered fisherman, along with an angler, is still with us.

Both sides of the river here have excellent footpaths, so take your time and enjoy it, even under the shelter of an umbrella. The difficulty with time and enjoyment is, if you attain one you may not have the other. Any angler I have met along the river seems to be fortunate in having both.

It is with great credit that we should thank the co-operation of, not only the ministry (agriculture and rivers), but the farmers and Roe Anglers Association for the maturity created along the banks of the Roe.

Growing Pains along the Roe

During the formative years of the Roe Anglers Association major drainage schemes were advocated under government policies on the land in Ulster. These were grant aided and the rivers bore the brunt of receiving a drastic overhaul. The rivers of the Province would suffer a severe disfigurement in that all trees, shrubbery, vegetation – wild plants, reeds etc. would be torn from the verge of the riverbanks. The shallows or sand-beds would be excavated to form a stream of water contained within "canal walls" to receive the surplus field drain-water that before would have soaked in, in gradual ease, and hence there was no risk of flash floods coming down river.

Natural weirs along the river generated oxygenated water that the fish thrived on without obstructing the passage for fish travelling up stream – man made weirs on the other hand had to be built with these benefits to the fish in mind. The river Roe, thankfully, has an abundance of natural rock formations that enhance the quality of the water, although the drainage schemes took away the reeds and plants that also produce oxygen in the river.

The risk of pollution is still an issue from silage tank overflows or leaks similar to the flax production. When flax was a common product of the farmer the wash, when the lent dams were drained, was supposed to be collected in filter receptacles – this was an understanding between both farm policies and the fisheries. (The flax trade was scuttled by the introduction of man made fibres in the early 1950s although the old dams, of which a few still remain, are discretely hidden under willows and weeds.

Coleraine Chronicle 1950.

FARMERS!

FLAX WATER

Flax growers are reminded that under the fisheries (Flax Water) Act (Northern Ireland), 1947, it is an offence: -

(a) to steep or attempt to steep any flax in any river or lake;

(b) to allow flax water to run or flow into any river or lake between 1st June and 30th November, inclusive;

(c) to allow flax water, which is poisonous to fish, to run or flow into any river or lake between the 1st December and 31st May, inclusive.

The Act also requires every person steeping flax to provide adequate means (e.g. catch dams) of disposing of flax water. Such persons may apply to the Flax Section, Ministry of Agriculture, Stormont, Belfast, for a certificate to the effect that the means provided are adequate. This certificate will be considered a defence in any case where a flax grower is prosecuted for not providing adequate means of disposing of flax water.

For providing such means, financial assistance up to 75 per cent of the cost may be given. Applications for such assistance should be addressed to the Ministry of Agriculture, Land Improvement Section, 32 Hopefield Avenue, Belfast.

Issued by the Ministry of Agriculture, Northern Ireland.

The areas worst affected by drainage schemes are from Deer Park to the mouth of the river, to prevent floodwater destroying the crops, and the flat land around the Gelvin and Bovevagh as well as Myroe. The meadows languishing around Pellipar are also susceptible to over flowing floods and here the river is contained within clay dykes. The 1830 Ordinance Survey tells us about the damage caused by voluminous floods driving through Aghanloo and Ballymaglin devouring crops, sheep, cattle and the very earth that guided the river. Due to the dredging and dyke construction ventures the character not only of the river but also the surrounding landscape is intruded upon. The comparison between natures formation guiding the water at the Green Bridge and Carrick, for instance, and the dykes in Myroe is evidence enough that man can not emulate nature.

The river Roe has carved its course out of carboniferous sandstone that extends in a long lobe under the basalt scarp from Dungiven northward. Near Limavady the river encountered a tougher substance in the schist between the Carrick Rocks and the Green Bridge and these are the areas that we delight in visiting most.

The fishing hook came with the inventive Bronze Age, however Stone Age man had been using implements - like the trident - constructed by using a simple piece of timber. The fishing net also dates from the Bronze Age.

This poem is from the Carrick and was written in 1899.

As I go over the Carrick Bridge

As I go over the Carrick Bridge,
In the amber light of dawn,
The fresh leaves whisper silkily,
Like the tread of the fleeting fawn.
And the mists appear,
Like genial queer,
Where the deep wet hallows yawn.

Under the bridge with a soothing lisp,
The soft dark waters flow,
The tall firs curve their shapely tops,
As breezes come and go.
Mosses and reeds,
And river weeds,
Along the margin grow.

The busy farmers seek the fields,
When the long days labours planned,
And just beyond the broken stile,
I see them cross the land.
And one is there,
With auburn hair,
Who waves her snow-white hand.

The gladdening sunbeams through the trees,
The bridges beams adorn,
On every side the Mayflower grow,
And the cuckoo birds are born,
Our land has not,
A sweeter spot,
Than the Carrick Bridge at morn.

The old Sluice, on the left of this painting, is redundant. This was a lead to power one of the mills further down the river years ago. It is one antique of the Roe bank that dwells in harmony, almost, with the surrounding trees - at least the reflection on a calm day becomes more intriguing with its rustic colours and contrasting texture.

The central theme, which is not apparent without a knowledge of what lies beyond, is the weir. The situation here is like one of those dreams were you find yourself falling – grasping – or simply a roller-coaster, but here is a subdued physical power, the water. A full appreciation of the weir is gained from the lower view-point a little further down the river, from the east bank.

The advantage with this walk is that you could park your car either at the Country Park or up here at the Carrick Flats and enjoy both sides of the river due to the bridges.

This painting was taken from the Gravel bed just upstream from the Green Bridge, in the townland of Largy. The area has been carefully manicured and the creation of parking spaces for the disabled as well as tourists, anglers, poets and painters is being taken advantage of. A slow gradient path leads to the river bank, where a sheltered seating pergola offers a recluse on a very wet day. To witness the force of a full flood coming down the Roe here is a comfortable corner from which to observe it and there is no doubt you will find a talkative local to idle the eddies around. The river takes a sharp turn at this point and the Rivers Department have eased the erosion of the banks by building with care a rock face.

As the name suggests the bed of the river is a mixture of sand, gravel, and rocks that offer a firm footing to the keen angler.

These verses are from the pen
of Samuel Connor, The Largy Poet.

The approach of Spring

Rejoice, my soul, exulting sing!
Oh! Feel'st thou not the breath of Spring,
The Springtime's balmy dawn.
Again, with warblers of the wood,
Pour out thy songs of gratitude,
As life goes rolling on.

Whose heart would not with rapture fill,
When spring, returning calm and still,
And darksome Winter's gone,
When woods resume their crown of green,
When life's on every aspect seen,
And lilies deck the lawn.

Again, his gratitude, the thrush,
Sings out upon the budding bush,
In tones beyond compare.
And peeping up with starry face,
By many an unfrequented place,
The primrose blushes fair.

Within his native grove, the dove,
Once more sings out his tale of love,
And through his changed retreat.
Once more the rapid swallow soars;
On high the lark his love-song pours,
In tones of rapture sweet.

Oh, see! Once more the willow tree,
Encompassed by the humming bee,
His brilliant garments wears;
The violet's face once more is seen,
And from his smiling bed of green
The little daisy stares.

Once more by forest, moor and dale,
The cuckoo's mellow voice we hail;
Oh! Let us grateful be,
Rejoice – in exultation sing,
For all the countless gifts of Spring,
A sweet doxology.

The old Carrick Mill a few years ago.

Visualise a young lady, about fourteen years of age, taking a stroll on a sunny afternoon down the braes of Leek. Leek is on the south-west bank of the river Roe, about six miles from Limavady. She has her father's shotgun, carried in a normal breech over her arm, the cartridges homed. A fox makes a break through the hawthorn hedge, to the right across the field. The youthful eyes and responses of this teenager are quick. The gun is cocked, aimed and fired without hesitation and before the report echoes from the beech trees, among the hawthorn hedge, the fox is prostrate not far from the Leek burn.

Amy, the tomboy, keen on all the activities that prevail in the rural community of Bovevagh in these post war years, collects the carcass and walks back up the brae for home. In the farmyard she leaves the gun propped against the shed wall and the fox beside it. A knife is required for the next task she has in mind. With the aid of her mother, the pelt is quickly stripped and scraped, with a liberal amount of saltpetre rubbed into the raw looking hide. Then with a few nails the fox skin is tacked to the shed door that catches the strong sunlight. A cup of tea, her mother suggests, and after washing their hands they both sit down at the kitchen table to enjoy a biscuit.

One thing that is profusely noticeable and invigorating about living in the country is the individual odours that are produced by efforts in cooking or cleaning out the cow shed or the sweet smell of the sally tree swaying in the breeze. One little lad noticed immediately a strange smell as he came around the gable end of the shed next to Amy's home – he was agitated now. The little terrier sprang and retrieved the fox hide with a vengeance – dead or alive he did not care – ripping and stripping and in no time the yard was dotted in orange – brown fur.

The sight, as Amy and her mother came out of the house to investigate the ruckus, was a shock and surprise but there stood a happy terrier.

This is the game young lady that would in later years marry Cyril Connolly.

' Salmon taken in close season '.

Fishery Prosecution at Dungiven – policeman's find in wood.

Before Mr. P. S. Bell, R. M., at Dungiven Petty Sessions on Friday 11th March 1949.

G….. K…, water bailiff, Bovevagh, summoned G….. McC……, Ardinarive, Dungiven for on the 18th January at Bonnanaboigh, having in his custody or possession a salmon wilfully caught in Bovevagh river during the Annual Close Season; also for using illegally a gaff for purpose of taking the fish from the river.

L….. M….., Caminish, Dungiven was summoned for aiding and abetting in each case.

Mr. W. S. McDermott prosecuted on behalf of the Fishery Conservators and Mr. W. J. D. Seeds appeared for the defendants.

Police Constable Fay had seen the two men come away from the bridge – he examined the area and found a spent salmon with gaff wounds still bleeding.

The water bailiff said he and another bailiff had concealed themselves near the river on the morning in question and saw the defendants twice near the bridge where there was a spawning bed.

With all evidence and defence heard his Worship said he had no doubt whatever that the defendants were the gentlemen who had the salmon in their possession and used a gaff. One of the defendants already had a previous conviction.

He was fined £2 and costs in each case – the other man was fined £1 in each case. One guinea extra costs was allowed in each of the four cases.

The construction of this old simple bridge is to be marvelled at, spanning from rock to rock using the same material, and each arch rests on the rock of the riverbed. The river can make no escape here, but the water laden with sand, especially during floods, has eroded a smooth face on its keeper.

The road down to the Bridge from the west is opposite The Gallows Hill, which is in the Townland of Ardgarvan, *Ard-gairbhean, the gravelly height or hill.* On the Largy side of the bridge, the east, the Country Park offers an array of interests – the café and natural history room display, as well as a large museum, in one of the old flax industry sheds, that contains a number of local artefacts that are worth studying.

Again the diligent efforts of all concerned locally have generated an area for all the family to enjoy.

This view of the Green bridge was painted from down river looking upstream. I am afraid the location is not accessible to the disabled or older person. However there is a platform created by the parks department from which to observe the flow of water over the rocky bed. Access to this platform is gained from the main road and path. The bridge is located in the Largy townland and part of an enjoyable days outing.

The painting offered a challenge with the contrasting rock textures and cascading water leaping in patterns, sometimes under strong sunlight and then perhaps in shrouded shadows. To determine the difference between foliage and rock is not important as the impression is reminiscent of French Impressionist Seurats techniques in painting where the completed scene requires no solid definition.

Limavady Petty Sessions. November 8th 1910.

Held on Tuesday before Messrs. J. D. Boyd (Presiding), G. B. Butler, R. M. Samuel Cassidy, Henry Connell and Mark B. Church.

Joseph Allen, water bailiff, summoned Thomas Tate, Limavady, and John Martin, Drumballydonaghy, for having had a gaff in their possession with intent to take fish.

There was a further case against Martin for assault on William Scott, a water bailiff from Rathbradymore.

Martin and Tate were defended by J. E. Proctor. --- W. S. McDermott for the complainants.

William Scott stated he saw the pair at the Roe in the townland of Killane on 29th October 1910. Thomas Tate inserted a stick with a gaff attached into the Roe as John Martin held his legs. They got no fish. William Scott and Joseph Allen rushed out but Tate ran away, dropping the stick but taking the gaff with him.

Scott chased after Tate but did not catch him. Scott went back and asked Martin why Tate ran. Martin said he did not know if it was Tate. Words not to be recorded were exchanged – a bit of slaging on both sides because Martin caught hold of Scott by the arm and said he would throw him in the river Roe.

The magistrates fined each of the defendant's £4 and John Martin was fined a further 10s. for the assault on William Scott.

During the floods in October 1898 a gentleman from Limavady put pen to paper and gave us this refrain, he called it…

An Old Song

It rose in cadence sweet and clear,
That old familiar song.
And sounds from many a bygone day,
Came to me 'mid the throng.

In it I heard the summer breeze,
That stirred the rustling leaves,
Along the winding glens of Roe,
On bygone tranquil eves.

In it I heard the reapers song,
Upon a harvest day,
In it the skylarks notes again,
Along the Keady brae.

I heard the ploughman's merry tune,
From uplands far away
The whetting of the mowers scythe,
Mid swathes of new mown hay.

I also heard the ringdoves croon,
The robins liquid note,
The plovers cry adown the glen,
Where broad-leaved lilies float.

I heard the brown bees browsy hum,
O'er the flowers of red and gold,
I heard from lips for ever mute,
The tender words of old.

In it again I heard, Ah! Me,
The church bells mournful sound,
The rustle of the tall rank grass,
Above a humble mound.

But joy and grief and hopes and fears,
That to the past belong,
Come back to fill mine eyes with tears,
By that old familiar song.

Fisheries - Board of Conservators. 1877.

Ireland Revenue Licences and Duties.

Licence – duties imposed by Act of 11 & 12Vic., c.92, on the various implements used in taking of Salmon in Ireland.

    No. 1. Single salmon rods….. £1.

    No. 2. Cross lines and rods…..£2.

    The licence for a drift net……£3.

The 21st section of the 11th & 12th Vic., c.92, exempts from duty rods used singly for taking trout, perch, pike or other fish except salmon.

    No. 12   Head weir….£3.

    No. 13. For every box, crib, cruive or drum net in any weir for taking salmon or trout…£5.

July 7th 1900

Robert Rodgers - rented the fishing distance of the Roe. He found that his expense was barely covered by the poor returns - He offered a reward of £1 to anyone bringing him any nets found in the river. One net was found hidden some distance below the town, by an unknown man, who claimed the reward.

Within Dear Park you will find and know why it was originally called, *the garden of the soul, Gort-na-anama.* Through the tree-lined paths you will come upon an area marked Kanes Rock and it is here that O'Cahans castle once stood. It was taken apart, bit by bit, shortly after Sir Thomas Phillips came to occupy this valley.

To view the scene in the painting it is necessary to get onto the east bank of the river and this is via the fortunate footbridges located close by. The scene itself is intriguing to paint because of the reflections depending on sunlight and the absence of wind. On each occasion upon visiting the scene you will find the aspect changed due to conditions and seasons. It would be tempting to invite and encourage a sever flood to carry away the trees and foliage that conceals a great part of O'Cahans Rock.

O'Cahans Rock in this painting is so draped in foliage that the rocks are not discernible however they form a backdrop to the main event, which is the motion of water over the artificial weir. The riverbed is dappled with rock and the banks are stoutly guarded by the same variety of massive stones. Projecting out of the water, except during floods, these rocks seem to be arranged to our advantage to use as stepping stones from which to view or to the benefit of the angler.

The footpaths offer a wide scope, following the undulating curvatures of the banks, with sympathy, and the aspects sustain that fine quality that the river Roe is famed for. Where man once used the water for power (the old laid on the left bank) is left unchanged and the undergrowth on the walks has merged it into the landscape in rustic terms.

Map 2 from the Green Bridge to the Mouth of the Roe.

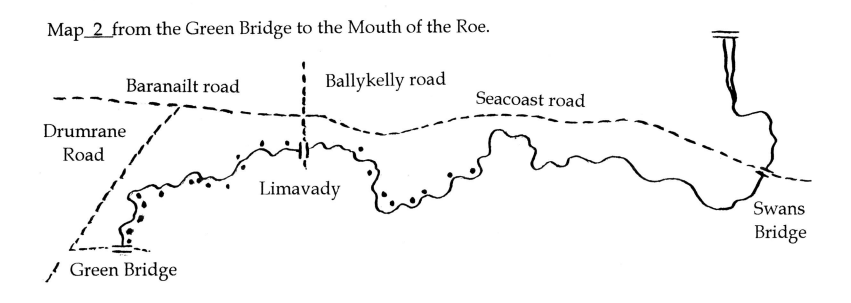

- PORTORS * LAMBS * KANES ROCK * THE COVE * BULLHOLE * JACKIES
- STAKEHOLE * BACKFALLS * ROEMILL * SPRING BRIDGE POOL * HYDROLIC RAM
- NEELEYS * BETTYANNS * LOWRYS * CATHERS * SOLDIERS HOLE * ST. HELENA
- BROLLYS * PATCHELLS * PEAT STACK * LADDIES HOLE * RABBIT BRAES
- MEETINGS * RACK * NEW CUTTING * RED BERRY

The pools are marked in descending order from the Green Bridge down river.
The map is based on Cyril Connollys 1950 maps and as you can see the lower pools are Absent.

All the water that accumulates in the river Roe is the product of the hills that shed their tears down their cheeks - our Dungiven poet expresses some other sentiments that we humans enjoy.

McSparrin

McSparrin, McSparrin, though the green sod long covers,
Thy moulding remains in an unsought for land.
Thy spirit still hovers at night with the plovers,
And broods o'er the rocks of thy sweet Carninban.
It wings through the air to Benevenny's green mountain,
And circles Lough Swilly with angelic speed,
And it's back in a twinkling by Curlys bright fountain,
Where thy witches rode races on elfin benweed.

It mourns o'er O'Kaghan and peeps at his castle,
Then pensively strays by the dark rolling Roe.
Like a shadow of moonlight 'neath the birches and nestle,
To watch the night poacher who fishing will go.
It visits each pool of thy dearly loved river,
Where the halo of romance cast by thy pen,
Time cannot alter, nor distance e'er sever,
The glamour thou shed over valley and glen.

Perhaps as I list to the burst of storm anguish,
That madly careers o'er the Bennedy plain,
To gather fresh force round Benbradagh will languish,
Is the wild 'cronie' cry of the spirit in pain.
Sleep peacefully, spirit, though this weak hand does venture,
To wipe from thine eyes this one solitary tear.
There's pens if they choose to make you their thoughts centre,
Thy down trodden laurels can raise, never fear.

Though there's no marble mound marks thy homestead, Drumrammer,
No 'storied urn' records Drumsurns pride.
The fragrance of 'thyme' still the kine does enamour,
Is thy silent tombstone on the Keadys hillside.
But of, for a loan of thy heaven sent treasure,
For a fraction of time while I pen down my lays,
That I might impart but one tenth of the pleasure,
To others you gave – to my own boyhood days.

Navigational proposals for the river Roe .....1690 and 1827

Limavady in 1690 was full of energy and enterprise with great expectations to develop the outlet for local produce. As you might expect, the roads were not of the quality that we use today and the 15 mile journey to the Derry market was a slow cumbersome undertaking. Broken springs, wheels and cart shafts made a four-hour trip a two day event waiting for smithy repairs. Because of all these hazards a plan was drawn up to develop the river Roe into a canal. The proposal was to straighten the river from Limavady to the townland of Granagh, and to continue on a 'cut' course through the "Myroe Gap" forming a line to where the branch railway line would eventually be laid. The canal was to enter Lough Foyle half a mile south of Widgeon Lodge. The railway line from Coleraine to Londonderry was completed and opened in 1853, many years after the canal proposal. The embankment at Ballymacran was under construction 40 years before the steam engines would pass by.

If this canal had been cut I wonder at the prospect of the Broighter Gold ever being unearthed, or buried even deeper. Or if found in 1690 where would it be now?

In 1827 a new proposal similar to the 1690 scheme was drawn up to shorten the distance to convey goods by barge. The natural course of the river from Limavady to the Roe mouth was nine miles and 116 perches. The new canal would leave Limavady only four and a half miles from Lough Foyle, where a terminal for loading and off loading goods from large ships would be created out in the deeper waters. The 1827 scheme was estimated to cost £12,155.

Neither of the above schemes ever materialised.

The variety of aspects to be enjoyed from the Glenshane all the way to Limavady make the river Roe unique. Here on the gentle braes that wander down to the river, from what was once an old peoples home and long before that the stately residence of the MacNaughtens, as well as other local gentry, are verdant greens.

Like a marathon runner, the surge and expended energy of the river is relaxed after its journey to slowly contemplate the reception from Mullagh Hill and Coolessan.

Away in the background Benbradagh seems to put on some airs and graces and so she might, sitting in her lofty plain.

From this location, along the river, there are natural compositions to inspire any artist to paint, whether he be an amateur or professional and the poet shall have his day. Mind you the banks have fierce thistles to contend with.

The view down the River Roe from an elevated plain under Mullagh Hill is tranquil, displaying a relaxed meadow. This small basin, long before the Celtic arrival, contained a proud expanse of water lapping Shanreagh townland bank on the left and Coolessan and Rathbrady Beg bank on the right. In 575 A.D. when Columba is supposed to have disembarked from his curragh at Mullagh Hill, to take part in the Drumceatt Convention, the river was a more refined affair.

After Columbas brief encounter with an Irish nobleman's scornful wife, her insults about his physical appearance, being lean, resulted in the local ford here being called the "herons ford". This ford is not used today, although the paths at either side are used to reach the river to fish.

This area is now a large golf course.

Twenty-five years after the famine a Limavady man gave us these few verses.

There is not in this Wide World a Valley so Sweet

Yes, there is in this wide world a valley as rare,
Where the streams run as clear and the flowers are as fair.
Where loves are as steadfast and friendships as true,
And the fair face of nature as lovely to view.

O, Moore for thy pencil this seems to portray,
As it ope's to the sight with the first blush of May.
Where the rising sun's beams gilds the rocks and the flood,
And the music rings out from O'Cahans old wood.

On the top of yon cliffs where the gnarled oaks grow,
Enraptured I've gazed on thy ripples fair Roe.
And I've thought that Avoca could scarcely compare,
With the beauty and grandeur surrounding me there.

Dear haunts of my boyhood, kind faces known then,
Some treasured and tried ones I may ne'er meet again.
But it lightens life's road as we journey on through,
To know we meet some friends kind-hearted and true.

A Limavady man wrote this poem in 1872. He was influenced by the Scottish Bard Rabbie Burns because the air he used was " Ye Banks and Braes of Bonnie Doon".

The River Roe

Oh, for the Ayrshire ploughman's muse,
Who sang so sweet of Bonnie Doon,
That I might paint our own sweet stream,
As seen at eve in a leafy June.

Its' sloping banks of brightest green,
Bedecked with natures fairest flowers,
And bashful youths and maidens coy,
Are slyly stealing through the bowers.

How sweet to stand upon the bridge,
To view the panoramic scene,
The river winding through Roe Park,
'Mid waving reeds and pastures green.

The troutlets slipping in the stream,
The swallows darting to and fro,
And noisy schoolboys shouts are heard,
Disporting in the pool below.

Oh, happy days! Oh, thoughtless boys!
Where are my loving schoolmates gone,
Away dispersed through other lands,
And still old Roe is speeding on.

Still murmuring on through fair Roe Park,
Careering round the Lodge Demesne,
And onward past the 'Castle Hill',
To join the 'Curly' at Killane.

So it will be in after times,
When ages shall have passed away,
And other men and other boys,
Shall on its sylvan margin stray.

They, too, shall hurry off the stage,
Like others who have gone before,
And Roe, fair Roe, pursue its track,
Still coursing onward to the shore.

More proposals for the river Roe that never materialised......1845.

Barges or boats, with a laden weight of 100 tons, were expected to be navigated up and down the River Roe after these proposals were instigated.

The 1845 proposal was to shorten the length of the river, similar to 1690 and 1827 proposals, and to cut through the embankments at Ballymacran into Lough Foyle. Obviously Mr. Robertson would have been interested in this venture to interrupt his dyke – "embanked sloblands". The river would adhere generally to the natural course that existed, a few 'cuts' would be made to straighten.

Two cuts to be made were – one from Granagh to Carbullion and the other from Ballyhenry West to Carrowmuddle. These cuts would shorten the river course by 3 miles and 67 perches. Embankments were to be created on either side by using the extracted riverbed which was to be deepened.

A new bridge was proposed for Magilligan and a new accommodation bridge to be built at Granagh/Carbullion to replace the ford which connects with the Lomond Road. A large sum of money was collected on hearing the proposal to expedite the construction of this bridge.

At the mouth of the river a sandbar was an obstacle formed by both silting from the river and the tidal waters of Lough Foyle. It was suggested that stone dykes would be formed in parallel lines 500 yds. apart and a channel would be dug out from the centre to a distance into the Lough that reached low water neap tides. The strength of fresh water currents from the Roe were to act as a scouring power and prevent the future formation of a new sand bar. The tidal waters were also expected to help scour the channel between these new stone dykes which were calculated to accommodate the rising tides.

Relaxed and lazy can describe both the river and the landscape here including Benevenagh in the background. At times you may be greeted by a pony on the other side of the style or even low flying golf balls. One hundred years ago there was no course here. However Limavady had golfers as the following few lines from the Irish Times in 1900 tells us: -

There was an irascible Paddy
Who hailed from remote
    Limavady,
He tore up the whin
That his golf ball lay in
And hamstrung his
    hiccoughing caddie.

   The poet also described another golfer with the lines:-

There was a young man from
    Belleck,
Who always approached with
    a cleck.
With a niblick he'd putt,
Use a spoon in a rut,
But his "waggle " was simply
    unique.

On the left bank of the river is the townland of Shanreagh, *Sean – Riaga, the old gallows,* also called, *Sean Riabhach,* by the nature of the soil, *the old grey land,* which is in the Parish of Tamlagth Finlagan. Spring Hill House, on the extreme right of the painting is in the townland of Rathbrady Beg, and just down river from Coolessan townland that features St. Columba's Spring opposite Mullagh Hill standing on the green behind Radison. It was on the Mullagh Hill that St. Columbas landed in 575 A.D. to contend with the bards over fees.

The other spring close to the Roe Bridge has not been given the same title but it is reputed that the Toberbrin spring travels from above Whitehill under ground to issue forth from the same area. Tober means spring, and brin is a well. Spring Hill House was the old police barracks.

In this 1901 poem from Limavady the poet reflects the energy of the season to come ......

Spring

Once more we hear the voice of spring,
In woodland, glen and grove,
The warblers cheer us with their song,
Wherever we may roam.
The banks break forth resounding,
And all nature seems in joy,
While the poet stands to paint the scene,
His pen he doth employ.

Once more the lark ascends on high,
His morning song to sing,
He loves to herald the morning's birth,
And herald the cheering spring.
Though oft he soars beyond our view,
We hear his notes sublime,
Like half-spent sounds borne on the breeze,
From some far distant clime.

Once more the bees have wakened from,
Their torpid winters dream,
They climb the golden ringlets of,
The willows by the stream.
Their feeble sounds so harmonise,
With other music strong,
The air seems tuned to melody,
To melody and song.

Once more we see the smile of spring,
It charms the wistful eye,
The sun sends down his golden rays,
From yonder placid sky.
The germs that sleep awake once more,
To clothe the naked ground,
While daisies variegate the fields,
And primrose decks the mound.

Once more the lesser celandine,
Adorns the river side,
These gems that tell of coming joys,
Most fitting for a bride.
These infant charms, nursed by the spring,
Point to maturity,
When summers flowery robes shall spread,
On mountain, glen and sea.

Once more we feel the scent of spring,
Rise from the fertile ground,
As natures' balmy breathing sends,
These healthy odours round.
For natures' casket now unseals,
And from her boundless store,
Our senses are all satisfied,
That spring's returned once more.

The following are a few more notes from Cyril Connolly's fishing diary.

July 1950 - Left at 8 a.m. with water just breaking into Pot Hole. Amy caught 6 lb. Salmon on the 'Flat' at about 12.30 p.m.

July 1950 - Albert Love got two salmon below Green Bridge on 1.1/2 spoon.

July 1953 - Watched Sand-martin bringing food to young.

7th June 1956 - First salmon of the year to L. McIlroy on spoon - 12lb. Cockfish. Sent away the 'scales' of this cockfish and confirmation to say that this was a Springer and our restocking was proving successful.

SPRING FRY MAKE GOOD.

Dear Sir,

I would appreciate readings from the enclosed two lots of salmon scales as I wish to know if they are spring fish. Our river has been restocked with spring fry for several seasons up to two years ago and it would be interesting to know if our experiment was bearing fruit.

Yours faithfully,

C. C. Connolly, Limavady, Northern Ireland.

W. G. Hartly has kindly sent us the following scale readings: -

"Mr. Connolly's fish were both small spring salmon. i.e. they were returning to spawn after two winters in the sea, Both had spent two years in the river before migrating as smolts, and in both cases the scales showed erosion amounting to 50 per cent of their margin - technically

termed three degrees of erosion, the scale margin being divided into six parts for purposes of assessment. This is to be expected in springers at this time of year, and shows that they are ripening to spawn. The length given with one of the fish marks it as a very fast grower; It did especially well in its first year at sea.

June 1956 - Alex Kealy 14lb. Fish

Aug. 1956 - Matthew Moore informed me that since our restocking program began to take effect The nets are getting salmon differing from the usual run of Roe fish.

Aug. 1956 - Owing to the increase in snatching at the Innler a committee meeting, by majority Vote, recommending to Foyle Commissioners that these weirs be put out of bounds. Brown, O'Hanlon, Stirling and Kealey voted against the matter. Surprised at Alex Kealey who gave me to understand that he was in favour of stamping out this practice. No doubt trouble will brew for the club and myself.

This twisting section of the River Roe is in the Parish of Drumachose, *Druim-An-Chiosa, the hill ridge of the tithes,* which is on the west bank, in the townland of Rathbrady Beg, *rath-Bhrighde-beag, the little fort of St. Brigid.* The painting was executed from the east bank, in the Parish of Tamlaght Finlagan, in an attempt to conceal the man-made dykes.

During a flood down the river the water can rise to considerable heights, and overflow the banks into the fields at an alarming rate. This experience is not often, but when it materialises you do not have to use your imagination to visualise a sublime invitation to sea-faring travellers.

St. Columba is reputed to have sailed past the shelf on which Limavady now rests to disembark at Mullagh Hill, one half mile up river - Why did he?

This view of Springhill House and the secluded Roe Bridge at the entrance to Limavady was painted from the townland of Lisnakelly, *Lios-na-coille, the fort of the woods,* in the parish of Tamlaght Finlagan. The complete radius of this corner of the river has endured a heavy assault from dredging over the years due to the fact that silt tends to settle on such bends. The sand bed where the fisherman is standing is known as the red bed by locals. Red is an obvious title to any part of the river because Roe in Irish, Rua, means red. Other explanations for the Roe name are: -

(a) a fish spawning bed "redd"
(b) an old Viking word 'hrogn' meaning fish roe. The Rua is the most obvious as the river mouth has an area long known as the Red Shoring, as well as other red beds along the river. Clay and sandstone elements washed down river have a red hue when dried in the sun.

Sept. 1956 - Gaffed fish for Dr. Charlton at 8.30 a.m. His first on No.8 Red Shrimp at tail of Turn Hole.

Oct. 1956 - Arrived at Dales with Amy about 7.30 a.m. We left two tracks on the dewy grass under a cloudy sky, which gave promise of a very bright day. Dales middle looked in perfect condition with the water just lapping the top of the stones. Rods were hastily erected and my choice of fly was a No.6 Claret on the dropper and a No.5 J.S. D.H. Shrimp in the tail. NO OFFER. Crossed over at head of Dales middle to find myself in a jungle of brambles and bushes, to get to Emmersons. At Emmersons found low water. Fished down to Magilligins. Down to McClenaghans where I followed Amy down the pool after seeing a fish grassed by J. Macdonald. A few casts and impolite words from Amy who lost one.

This tale ends with Cyril foul hooking a fish that he played but could not bring to the bank. Cyril coaxed it under a tree where Amy gaffed it.

July 1966 - Got up early - waters very dark at 2+ - gave it the works to no avail and just could not fathom why the fish were not taking. Left and returned about 5 p.m. - Suddenly struck me that the fish were sickened with what must be bog water. Fished on and eventually got a sea trout. Went off to the 'Meetings' but the water was too heavy for night fishing. Peculiar antics at 10.30 p.m. from a salmon in the Glebe - out of the Meetings. It gave five or six terrific leaps all over the water - may have been pursued by an otter or it may have been affected by the disease which caused fish to leap madly around according to symptoms noted by Mallock. I hope this is not the case.

July 1966 - No offers other than the hand shake from my friend at 'The Rock'.

July 1967 Commenced fishing at 7 a.m. - John on water before me. Cast on sink-line No.5 D.H.R.S. tail, No.7 – J.S. Shrimp. Dropper (yellow/gold and black body ribbed to tinsel. Hot orange.....no centre hackle. Rhode Island Red front hackle). Killed 7.15 a.m. to dropper, best fish to same fly tail of Carrick Stream. Fished with this cast and changed to floating line and a cast with tall D.H.R.S.No.8 and No.6 for R.S. dropper without avail until 11.30 a.m. Changed back to sink line and single cast and had momentary contact with a fish below Carrick Rock to the dropper – J.S. This J.S. Shrimp looked redder and more natural in the conditions which appeared proper for catching fish. Fished intermittently and had two half-hearted offers half way down the Mill Stream. 4.20 p.m. changed the position of the flies in the cast. No offer in Pot of Carrick Stream. Got flush at head of Carrick Stream, fished it very carefully and killed fish half way down to the J.S. Shrimp. No further offers. Rain commenced 6.30 p.m.

July 1967 - Met Jim Adams at supper with Herbie McIlwaine - he fishes nothing but the worm across the 'Meetings'. He is to let me know whether his experiments are successful with a concoction fed to the worms......Very secret!

To what meals the woods invite me
    All about!
There are water, herbs and cresses
    Salmon, trout.

Bees and Beetles, music makers
    Croon and strum.
Geese pass over, duck in Autumn
    Dark streams hum.

From the Irish Hermits Song - 7th century.

The Irish Wolfhound (1660)

Behold this creature's form and state!
Him nature surely did create,
That to the world might be exprest,
What mien there can be in a beast.
More nobleness of form and mind,
Than in a lion we can find.
Yea, this heroic beast doth seem,
In majesty to rival him.
Yet he vouchsafes to man to show,
His service, and submissive too,
And here we a distinction have.
That brute if fierce – the dog is brave.
He hath himself so well subdued,
That hunger cannot make him rude.
And all his manners do confess,
That courage dwells with gentleness.

This is another view of the Red bed, painted on a wet day, because I enjoy the different light of clouded, threatening skies. Perhaps the sun breaks through the cloud now and again invigorating the sodden green hues of the riverbank, against a golden autumn field in the vicinity.

The evidence that justifies the townland name where we stand in this painting, Lisnakelly, *the fort of the woods,* is partially visible from the main Ballykelly road. The woods on the right, along the road, have receded due to agricultural demand over the years, and is now shyly hid behind Lisnakelly ridge. " The Rough Fort "stands proudly among the few remaining sentinels of beech trees. The old townland names give more information about the character of each area, which would justify their use in postal addresses.

There are two directions to reach the site from which this painting was completed and they are both difficult. The first is from the old railway station going down river on the west bank, where you will encounter an abundance of thistles, little wonder they germinate elsewhere. The other approach is from down river with a long walk from the Curly Bridge, but you have to cross the Castle Burn on your way. Obviously it is not an area of easy access which is very disappointing.

The townland at this section of the river is in Killane, *Coill-leathan, the broad wood,* in the parish of Drumachose. The definition of the townland name gives us a far idea of what the rural setting was like centuries ago.

Drumballydonaghy, *Druim-baile-ui-Dhonnchaidh, the ridge of the townland of the O'Donaghys,* is on the right bank.

Along The River Roe

Sam Connor wrote this poem about ' Granie's Bed ', the bed of the banshee of the O'Cahans, situated near Benbradagh. Sam Connor was only fourteen when this poem was printed.

Let others boast of foreign climes,
And vales beyond the sea;
I do not doubt in distant lands,
Are fairy scenes to see;
But give to me a pleasant stroll,
When summer's breezes blow,
Where the primrose stars the verdant banks,
Along the river Roe.

Oft have I trod its flowery banks,
Its fertile valleys through;
Its woodlands green, and bonnie braes,
Sweet natures charms to view.
Where will you meet with foreign scenes,
No mater where you go,
To rival the historic scenes,
Along the river Roe.

Upon its banks there stands a rock,
Surrounded by a wood,
Upon its lofty summit once
O'Cahans castle stood.
There travellers go to mediate
On days of long ago,
When the chieftain chased the shaggy wolf
Along the river Roe.

No more the place is glistening now
With swords of warlike men,
No more is heard the chieftains horn
Resounding through the glen.
Where front their beds of verdure green
The fragrant bluebells grow.
Yet tourist praise that beauteous spot
Along the river Roe.

The dipper perched with snowy breast
Among the sparkling spray,
There mingles with the torrents roar
His low melodious lay.
There dose the grand kingfisher oft,
His matchless plumage show,
There loudly thrills the moorhens note
Along the river Roe.

How gaily stand the Carrick Rocks
Where travellers love to roam,
Within the clefts the jackdaws build,
The kestrel makes his home.
In olden days the fairies there
Went sporting to and fro,
There still remain their rocky caves,
Along the river Roe.

There dose the angler love to rove
Where lusty salmon spring,
Where in surrounding woodlands gay
The feathered poets sing.

The waiting rock dove haunts that scene
Whose ivy mantles glow
That bears the little Parish Church
Along the river Roe.

There you can see old " Granie's Bed "
Upon the rocky height;
There still they say, in loneliness
She rambles yet by night.
At times benighted travellers hear
Her dismal tale of woe,
As she wails for some descendant's death
Along the river Roe.

Now tyrant hearts, far foreign climes
Go visit if you will,
But leave your hearts by ' Granie's Bed ',
Cahans Rock and Gallows Hill.
Think on the scenes of boyhood days,
Where sparkling waters flow,
And don't despise your native plains
Along the river Roe.

The only remains of McKays old Plantation, that covered the high ridge on the west bank of the river here, is a hedge that constitutes hawthorns, ash trees and surprisingly a few apple trees that still do bear fruit.

I painted this scene on two separate occasions, both during the afternoon, with the sun shinning down river through broken clouds. Over the partially submerged stepping stones the light on the water required a snap decision on colour or brush stroke to capture its ever changing mood.

On the east bank is Ardnargle and the west bank is in Killane townland. This area is relaxed because the few anglers that you might encounter are secluded close to the waters edge and tourists seldom venture to walk these banks.

" The meetings " - you would expect a more romantic complexion to the confluence than that which is evident where the Castle Burn unites with the river Roe, in the townland of Clooney, *Cluainte, the meadows,* in the Aghanloo Parish. The Castle is joined with another burn, the Curly, in the townland of Gortnamoney, *Gort-na-mona, the tilled field of the bog,* also in Aghanloo Parish. These waters, the Roe, Castle and Curly quietly meet and pass the banks at Ardnargle, *Ard-n-aireagal, the high Oratory or the hermits cell.*

The high earth dykes are necessary in this area when severe floods come down the river. The banks impede the visibility of the landscape on this stretch of the river, however Benevenagh still manages to keep an eye on us from a distance. It is a quiet place for a days fishing.

J. McCrory, who once lived in Bolea, *Buaile, the lea of the milking cow,* returned to the Curly from his new home in Melbourne in 1905, after many years' absence, with these words.

The Curly Burn Revisited

Along the green banks of the old Curly Burn,
Many years have elapsed and now I return,
To see and to meet the old friends at last,
To think and to muse on the days that are past,

The bubbles that float down thy course,
And whirl along with varying force,
Remind us of our sojourn here,
Through storm and sunshine in the year.

How many on thy banks have stood?
To watch thee in thy wintry mood,
How many, too, in summer time,
Have fought their fight and drunk their wine.

At present time and days of yore,
With change of fate and hearts full sore,
Yet all the time with motive bent,
To find in something hearts content.

It may have be a foe to kill,
More honestly a field to till,
Yet each and all to gain a prize,
By earthly means through human eye.

On thy banks lovers have strolled,
In autumn and in winter cold,
Under shade of sunbeams ray,
Love, joy, peace and ecstasy.

The silent Keady hills around,
Oft have heard the battle sound,
Whilst quiet and secluded spots,
Have sheltered many family cots.

Remember then, O foolish man,
Change and decay destroy our plan,
We build our castles very strong,
The torrent comes and sweeps along.

Leaving our habitations bare,
Withal our skill, withal our care,
Alas the changes everywhere,
The old have gone, the young and fair.

Yet time has not much changed thy face,
On goes thy rocky rapid race,
Thy rippling waters flow forever,
Though friendship fails and death do sever.

The loved ones who have crossed life's stream,
With love, with hope - " Life's But a Dream "

_____

This poem was noted from a Limavady man in November 1897.

A Good - bye to Summer

The bright young life of spring has gone,
   Fled are the flowers of May.
Green summers leaves are falling fast,
   And yellow by the way.

Cold wailing winds come creeping on,
   To herald winters chill.
The swollen river rushes past,
   Mists move along the hill.

No more the choir from wood and glen,
   Sends forth the gladdening strain.
No more the joys of tranquil eve,
   For autumns on the wane.

We must forego the gladsome days,
   And sights we late have seen.
When all the world was richly dressed,
   In royal robes of green.

Farewell ye mountains heather crowned,
   Good-bye to sunny glade.
Adieu, ye meadows where I've strolled,
   At evenings deepening shade.

Good-by ye hazel banks and glens,
   Through which the Curly flows.
Ye'll soon be held within the hush,
   Of natures cold repose.

And now to wait with patient hope,
   And count each passing day.
Till sleeping beauty shall arise,
   And springs sweet voice obey.

When an exile returned for a visit to his old home in Aghanloo, in 1898, his heart gave vent to the following poem.

Sweet Aghanloo

O, Aghanloo, sweet Aghanloo,
Thy green hills fair I see.
Full many a dream of yon fair spot,
My memory brought to me.
But now I wear thy flowers fair,
As ever nature grew,
The scented thorn that still adorn,
The braes of Aghanloo.

The verdant plains to me appeared,
In midnight reverie,
Again I heard the warblers sing,
Their notes in every tree,
For gay had been my boyhood scene,
And pleasing to review.
No care oppressed my youthful breast,
In thee, dear Aghanloo.

Between thy bonnie winding hills,
And fertile plains below,
A murmuring river onward rolls,
We always call the Roe.
With rod and line I've passed the time,
Each day an hour or two,
Along that stream where beauties beam,
In the sweet Aghanloo.

Time has not changed the aspect much,
Of thy dear glens and hills,
But when we gaze o'er boyhood's days,
Our heart with sorrow fills.
For those we've lost and valued most,
Has from our presence flew.
They rest within the churchyard grey,
In dear old Aghanloo.

We sigh for scenes and days now gone,
And friends now called away,
With whom we spent in sweet content,
Full many a pleasant day.
They're gone the way all humans go,
And soon I'll follow too,
But unto death I'll not forget you,
Long-loved Aghanloo.

This secluded profile of Benevenagh is from Carbullion, *carr-chuillin, rocky land of the holly,* in the parish of Aghanloo, *Athan-Lugha, the little ford of Lugh.* Aghanloo is named after one of the mythological Irish Celtic gods retaining the old Druid elements – sun and light – and also the god of arts and crafts from his guardianship over the Tuatha De Danaan.

The otter, thankfully, are still evident along the banks of the river Roe - perhaps a few of the fishermen would prefer their absence during the active season of the salmon and trout 'run'.

When heavy clouds shed their burden over the Glenshane, experience has induced man to embrace the lower flat plains where the Roe flows between dykes to protect the rich farmland. The land between Aghanloo and Lough Foyle is the most fertile soil in the barony of Kennaught.

In the townland of Cressy Crib, situated in the Aghanloo Parish, the surrounding landscape is flat and seems to form a base for Benevenagh to rest upon. Cressy Crib, *craosach-gcrib, the gluttony of the shaking bog,* is adjacent to Crindle and these two areas have suffered the tantrums of the untamed river Roe. The juvenile river, many years ago, wanted to wander at will over these two townlands, but man decided otherwise and curtailed her within the banks. The twists and turns of the river were an advantage to the flax growers who were able to siphon of and discharge surplus water back to its source the Roe. This was close to Baron Martins home, Crindle House, and when the Rural District Council began to build new cottages in 1900 for the farm labourers the sites were situated close to these dams. A new course was cut to direct the Roe away from their homes.

These are the recorded thoughts of a Limavady man, upon the River Roe in April 1906.

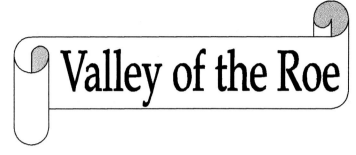

Valley of the Roe

A scene of soft enchantment,
Whose potent magic spell,
Might soothe this rude worlds' dissonance,
There in the dreamy dell.
The soul drinks inspiration,
While fancy murmurs low,
'Tis Eden sure in miniature,
This Valley of the Roe.

Enchanted I followed the pipes of Pan,
Through sylvan glades, as sweet notes ran,
Rythmical soft and low,
The love god thrilled to the elfin train,
Through the Valley of the Roe.

O, 'tis a scene transporting,
To be remembered long,
The songsters of the woodland fill,
The balmy air with song.
The haze of golden glory floods,
The ample vale below,
'Tis Eden sure in miniature,
This Valley of the Roe.

What hand hath carved yon rocky steps,
Magnificently vast,
Which terminate the mountain ridge,
Where storied Foyle flows past.
They seem as meant for gods to climb,
When visitants below,
Crowning my dream of Eden,
With this Valley of the Roe.

The Swans BRIDGE
From 1900 ...

Two Parishes, Magilligan and Tamlaghtfinlagan, *MhicGiollagain and Tamhlacht-Fionnlogain,* share the river as a boundary under the " rock " face of Benevenagh, standing 1260 feet above sea level. Scotchtown and Bellarena, *baile-albanach and beal-atha-riona,* the townlands embrace the left bank dressed with a variety of elm, sycamore, beech and ash tree.

Icebergs carried the old bridge away in winter. On the 14th July 1800 the masons, carpenters, builders and the local people held a grand dance to open the new bridge, known to the locals as Swans bridge. The pipe music of the 'Kilmary' family entertained the enthusiastic gathering till long after daybreak.

The Bellarena estate, once the old residence of Sir John Haygates and the Gages, nestles among the trees on the left.

The Keady, *Ceids, the flat topped mountain,* viewed over the townland of Ballycarton, Croaghan and ballyleighery (upper), *Baile-Cearcha, Cruachan and Baile-ui-Laeghaire,* all in the parish of Magilligan, was painted from the site of the old demolished bridge.

Assist me in my merriment,
Attend both one and all,
Till I relate the accidents,
At the Ballycarton Ball.
Like other lads my heart was
     sad,
For missing of the spree,
But I can tell the troubles there
When Betty lost her knee.
It was a noble gathering,
As far as I do know,
From Aghanloo and
     Magilligan,
And far up in Myroe......

The Ballycarton Ball was composed in 1876 by James McCurry, the blind fiddler, from Myroe.

FROM NATEIKE
RESERVE AT
THE ROE MOUTH.

111

The east bank on the mouth of the river, down in Myroe, is in the townland of Carrowmuddle, *Ceathru-modh-dala, the quarterland of the Court of the Dail.* The bridge conveys the railway line that was constructed in 1850, in conjunction with a reclamation programme to develop the shoreline into rich farming ground. The Roe flows into Lough Foyle at this point.

Reference: -

The Ulster Way – Northwest Section.
County Londonderry Handbook (D. McCourt).
Irish Association for Quaternary Studies (Field Guide No. 7) Northwest, Co. Londonderry.
The Land of the Roe – S. Mitchell.
Notes on Place Names, Co Londonderry. Alfred Munn. 1925.
Sentinel – Microfilm 1910.
Coleraine Chronicle – 1877, 1898 to 1907, 1949 & 1951.
Thoms Almanac 1877.
Celtic Way of Life – O'Brien.
Maps Hand Drawn by Cyril Connolly 1950.
Interview with Mrs Amy Connolly – January 2000.
Cyril Connollys Roe Anglers Diary 1949 – 1968.

A very special thanks to Mrs. Connolly for her kindness in supplying me with Cyrils documents. I would also like to thank all the following businesses, in and around Limavady, without whose encouragement and financial support this book would not have been published.

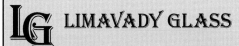

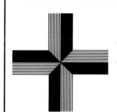

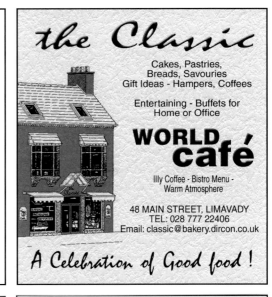

Victor McCurry was born in Carrowclare, Myroe, in 1948. He was educated at Limavady High School before going to Belfast College of Art. After teaching for a spell he decided to change his career and took up painting pictures full time. His paintings hang in many private collections, both locally and as far afield as Canada, America and Geneva.

Victor has been married to Deanna for nearly thirty years and he is the proud father of daughter Dallas and son Stephen, both living in Newcastle-Upon-Tyne. He also has a grandson Dylan, Dallas's son.

Victor has decided to combine his interest in local history with his love of the Roe Valley and this book which will be the first of many is the result.